NOOTKA SOUND IN HARMONY

Aborignal Conne

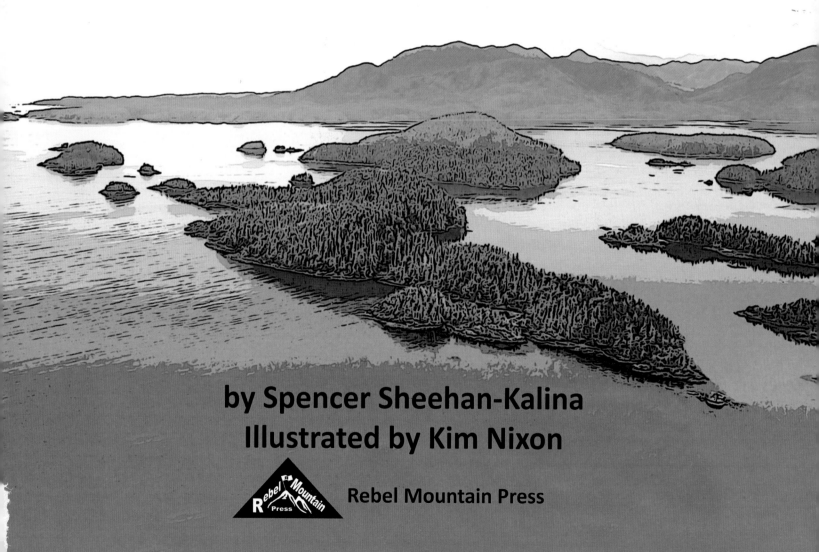

by Spencer Sheehan-Kalina
Illustrated by Kim Nixon

Rebel Mountain Press

Published by Rebel Mountain Press, 2019

Library and Archives Canada Cataloguing in Publication

Title: Nootka Sound in harmony : Aboriginal connections / by Spencer Sheehan-Kalina ; illustrated by Kim Nixon.
Names: Sheehan-Kalina, Spencer, 1991- author. | Nixon, Kim, 1991- illustrator.
Identifiers: Canadiana 2019009009X | ISBN 9781775301936 (softcover)
Subjects: LCGFT: Poetry.
Classification: LCC PS8637.H444 N66 2019 | DDC jC811/.6—dc23

All interior and cover illustrations by Kim Nixon
except pages14 & 15 - paintings by Kristyana Octavia Lastavec
pp: 1,7,26-Pixabay, pp 3,10,20,33,25,27 -Pxhere, pp-4,6,16,17, 24 -Wikipedia Commons
Special thanks to these school districts: Alberni, Comox, and Cowichan for sharing their resources.

Printed and bound in Canada by Marquis
Issued in print format:
ISBN 978-1-7753019-3-6 (bound)
Rebel Mountain Press—Nanoose Bay, BC, Canada
We acknowledge that we are located on the traditional territory of the Snaw-Na-Was First Nation

www.rebelmountainpress.com

part 1
Nootka Sound Paddling Song

Aboriginal Connections:

WHERE IS NOOTKA SOUND?

Nootka Sound is a beautiful inlet found on the west coast of Vancouver Island in British Columbia, Canada.

The first people to live there were Nootka First Nations (Mowachaht/ Muchalaht) people. Later, the fur traders and the lumber trade moved into Nootka Sound.

It is a magical and wonderful little spot that is sometimes called "Friendly Cove." The First Nations people and many different types of animals lived happily together in Nootka Sound. They lived in harmony.

There is nothing I'd rather do
on an early July morning
than spend some time in my canoe,
Nootka Sound's Paddle Song we'll sing!

Aboriginal Connections:

THE FIRST NATIONS PEOPLE IN NOOTKA SOUND

The Mowachaht/Muchalaht First Nations are a First Nations community that has lived on and around the area of Nootka Sound for thousands of years. When James Cook, the first explorer from England, sailed into the Mowachaht/ Muchalaht inlet, the villagers shouted to him "nuutkaa." James Cook thought they were shouting the name of the inlet, "Nootka," but they were really telling him to "circle around."

The First Nations wooden longhouses in Nootka were huge because they were home to several families. The houses were up to 30 metres (100 feet) long and 12 metres (40 feet) wide. That is bigger than a tennis court!

The main ceremony dance of the First Nations people of Nootka Sound was the wolf dance, also known as *"Tlugwana."* This is a wolf mask worn in the dance.

Down to the shore with canoe in tow,
Now it's time for paddling.
Off adventuring we go.
Nootka Sound's Paddle Song we'll sing!

Aboriginal Connections:

SEAWEED YOU CAN EAT!

Red laver is seaweed that looks a bit red and is found on the shoreline. It can be boiled with oolichan grease, fish, and clams to make a tasty soup.

The First Nations people also spread red laver on rocks in the sun to dry. When it was completely dried, it was chopped into pieces and eaten as a snack, like potato chips or cornflakes. Sometimes these dried pieces would be pounded into a fine powder, mixed with water and whipped until it was a foamy dessert treat.

You probably eat seaweed without knowing it. Agar, which comes from red laver, goes into candy, ice cream, and sherbet.

Off adventuring we go
past boats, nets, docks, and mill,
past where seaweed fingers grow.
Nootka Sound's Paddle Song we sing!

FOOD OF THE FIRST NATIONS IN NOOTKA SOUND

The Nootka First Nations got most of their food from the sea. They gathered clams, sea urchins, and mussels along the shoreline during low tide. They also caught salmon, halibut, cod, and herring along the coast. The fish was cooked in large wooden pots with water and hot stones, or dried so they could eat it later in winter.

The Mowachaht/Muchalaht First Nations people also collected plants from the land. They picked salal berries, salmonberries, blackberries, cranberries, wild crab apples, blueberries, and wild onions that tasted like sweet potatoes. The people made tea out of dandelions, and sore throat medicine out of licorice roots.

Indigenous Peoples never wasted anything. They made sure to never overfish, or take too many plants. They fished, and collected only what was needed to support their families.

Off adventuring we go
past seals, fish, gulls, and otters,
Paddling deep ocean, where orcas go.
Nootka Sound's Paddle Song we sing!

WHY DO ORCA WHALES JUMP OUT OF THE WATER?

A killer whale, or orca, has a lot of ways to talk with their family (pods). They hum, grunt, and even make special clicking noises to track or find food.

Sometimes, orcas make a big noise by slapping their tails or jumping in the air. When whales jump completely out of the water, it is called breaching.
An orca can jump between three metres (10 feet) to 4.5 metres (15 feet) out of the water. That is higher than a school bus!

Often, orca whales will breach in rough seas to breathe in air. Some orcas will jump in the air to make a big splash to knock a seal off a rock or piece of ice.

Off adventuring we go
to where orcas play
and do their acrobatic shows,
Nootka Sound's Paddle Song we sing!

Aboriginal Connections: ORCA WHALES

First Nations people and killer whales have lived in harmony in the Nootka Sound for many thousands of years. Killer whales, or orcas, are known as the king of the sea and it is believed that they protect the people of Nootka Sound. Orca whales live in pods, or family groups, that live and hunt together. Orcas take care of each other and always help and protect each other.

The Mowachaht/Muchalaht First Nations people also call the orca "wolf of the sea," or *kakaw`in*. Legend is that when the orca came ashore, he turned into a wolf, and the wolf became a protector of the Longhouse.

Off adventuring we go
with our new friends we play,
We're now part of their great show,
Nootka Sound's Paddle Song we sing!

WHO WAS LUNA?

Luna was the famous orca whale who was separated from his pod (family) when he was two years old. No one knew for sure why Luna came to live in Nootka Sound. Some of the Mowachaht/Muchalaht people believed that their leader who had died, Chief Ambrose Maquinna, had come back to them as a whale. They welcomed Luna and named him Tsu'xiit. Luna loved to play and made friends with everyone. He would rub against the side of a boat and swim with the slower boats, such as sailboats and tugs.

Off adventuring we go
with orca friends following close,
I even kiss one's giant nose!
Nootka Sound's Paddle Song we sing!

Aboriginal Connections:

The story of Luna continued:

Scientists were worried that Luna was getting too close to boats so they decided to get Luna to follow them back to his pod, away from Nootka Sound. The Mowachaht/Muchalaht people did not want Luna to leave. As the government ships tried to take Luna away, the Mowachaht/Muchalaht First Nations people paddled up in long canoes and sang songs. Luna followed the canoes back to Nootka Sound. The story of Luna and his friendliness continue to warm the hearts of everyone who hears it.

Now, a new adventure we know,
We return cold and tired, paddling slow
With our new friends in tow,
Nootka Sound's Paddle Song we sing!

Aboriginal Connections:

USE OF CEDAR

Nootka Sound First Nations used cedar to make canoes. They also used the bark of red and yellow cedar trees for rope, baskets, and clothing.

The people showed great respect for the cedar tree. Before they took any part of the tree, they would first say a prayer of thanks to the tree. They only took one long strip from one part of the tree and were very careful to not kill the tree. The bark would be torn into smaller strips then softened in water, soft enough to be woven.

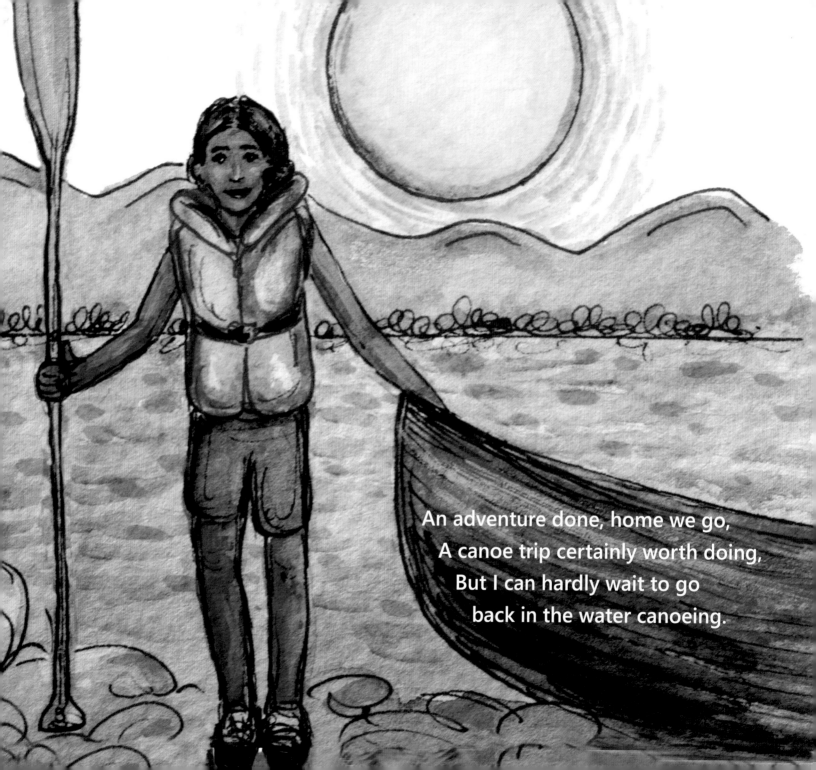

An adventure done, home we go,
A canoe trip certainly worth doing,
But I can hardly wait to go
back in the water canoeing.

Aboriginal Connections:

The First Nations people in Nootka spoke Nuu-chah-nulth. Here are the Nuu-chah-nulth words for these animals:

čims - black bear

waaxni- otter

kakaẃ'in- orca

kiłanuus- seal

ćixʷatin- eagle

Part 2

Animals in Nootka Sound

cuwit -coho salmon

Aboriginal Connections:

IMPORTANCE OF OOLICHANS

Oolichans were the first fish to come into Nootka Sound after the winter. These fish were a very important food for theMowachaht/Muchalaht First Nations people. The oil from oolichans was carefully stored for the entire year and used to make a type of butter. The oil was also used as a medicine to stop fever and earache, and it is also very good for the skin. After catching the oolichans, the First Nations people would eat some of the fish baked or fried. Most of the catch was sundried on cedar ropes or poles, or smoked over a fire so it could be stored for the year.

Oolichans are also a favourite food for eagles and they sit on the edge of the water waiting for the oolichans to arrive.

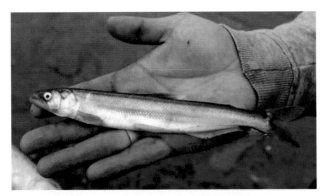

Oolichans are very small fish.

Eagle Mask

Oolichans

The oolichans! The oolichans!
They've come to visit us again
They sing, "Spring's here."
So now we can cheer,
for now we feast with no restrain.

Eagle

Like black kites scaling through the air,
the bald eagles begin to tear
off into the sky
so, so high, high, high,
and then nosedives to catch a hare.

Eagle catching oolichans

Aboriginal Connections: SALMON

A First Salmon Ceremony was held when the first large salmon of the year arrived. The people would sing songs and pray to the king of all salmon for sending the fish to the Mowachaht/Muchalaht people. The celebration could last up to ten days.

Most of the summer would be spent fishing by the river. Families would gather when the salmon came up the river and worked together to catch enough to feed everyone. They did not waste any part of the fish, and they kept all of the parts including the head, eyes, inside organs, and eggs. Salmon was saved for the winter by wind drying it on racks, smoking it over a fire, or by canning it.

The bears were also excited that the salmon had come up the river and they would eat as many as they could.

Otters

Look! There! An otter family
playing together, happily,
Shhh, watch them juggle,
dive, swim, and huddle.
Let's sit and watch them quietly.

Bears

All of the hungry bears want some
of the salmon that has come
home to find a mate.
Their fishing paws wait.
After, there's not even a crumb.

All about the author:

Spencer Sheehan-Kalina would like children to discover and learn in ways that are exciting, fun, and silly! He has written a number of quirky poems that celebrate the natural world and cultural heritage, which have appeared online and in print. Spencer is a member of the Maniwaki Metis Nation and was born in Ottawa, Ontario. He has lived in Gold River, close to Nootka Sound. Spencer now lives in Courtenay on Vancouver Island with his two cats.

You can read more of Spencer's poetry in these two books published by Rebel Mountain Press

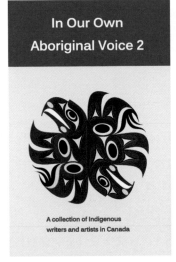

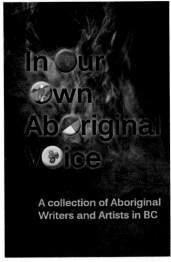

Parents and educators:

Please see this Rebel Mountain Press web page for more Aboriginal connections, online links, and videos.

www.rebelmountainpress.com/nootka-sound-links.html